DRUG DANGERS

STEROID DRUG DANGERS

Judy Monroe

Enslow Publishers, Inc.

44 Fadem Road   PO Box 38
Box 699   Aldershot
Springfield, NJ 07081 Hants GU12 6BP
USA   UK

http://www.enslow.com

Library of Congress Cataloging-in-Publication Data

Monroe, Judy.
    Steroid drug dangers / Judy Monroe.
        p.   cm.
    Includes bibliographical references and index.
    Summary: Discusses the short-term and long-term effects and dangers of steroid drug use, recounts the stories of various people who have abused them, and explains how to get help with this problem.
    ISBN 0-7660-1154-2
    1. Anabolic steroids—Health aspects—Juvenile literature.
2. Doping in sports—Juvenile literature. [1. Steroids. 2. Athletes—Drug use. 3. Drug abuse.] I. Title
    RC1230.M67   1999
    362.29'9—dc21   98-39942
                                                                          CIP
                                                                          AC

Printed in the United States of America

10 9 8 7 6 5 4 3 2 1

To Our Readers:
All Internet addresses in this book were active and appropriate when we went to press. Any comments or suggestions can be sent by e-mail to Comments@enslow.com or to the address on the back cover.

Photo Credits: © Copyright 1997, 1996 T/Maker Company, p. 14; Corel Corporation, pp. 7, 9, 10, 11, 12, 16, 20, 25, 52, 54; Díamar Interactive Corp., pp. 42, 46; New England Stock Photos, John and Diane Harper, p. 6.

Cover Photo: Corel Corporation, Enslow Publishers, Inc.

contents

17.88

austin

Titles in the **Drug Dangers** series:

Alcohol Drug Dangers
ISBN 0-7660-1159-3

Crack and Cocaine Drug Dangers
ISBN 0-7660-1155-0

Diet Pill Drug Dangers
ISBN 0-7660-1158-5

Heroin Drug Dangers
ISBN 0-7660-1156-9

Inhalant Drug Dangers
ISBN 0-7660-1153-4

Marijuana Drug Dangers
ISBN 0-7660-1214-X

Speed and Methamphetamine Drug Dangers
ISBN 0-7660-1157-7

Steroid Drug Dangers
ISBN 0-7660-1154-2

one

John's Story

John began bodybuilding when he was fifteen. Soon he became a prizewinning football star. A kind, gentle man, John knew he was a role model to his two children and to the dozens of young people at the gym where he worked out. So he ate healthful foods and never smoked cigarettes or drank alcohol. His marriage was strong, he had lots of friends, and he was admired by many people.

John did not know it yet, but at age thirty-five, he was very sick. And he had caused his own illness. What had he done?

After he turned thirty, John decided to try to keep his large, powerful body from aging.[1] He wanted to keep his muscular build and great strength. John weighed 220 pounds and stood six feet two inches tall. So for at least three years, he took anabolic steroids. The drugs were sold to him and others out of a suitcase.

John went to the gym every day. After he opened his locker, he would take out his drugs and equipment and find a private place to inject himself with anabolic steroids. Then, he would work out and help other athletes and teens. One friend, Bob, remembers that when John would first see him, John always shouted the same thing: "Hi Bob; when're you gonna let me show you how to put some muscles on that skinny body of yours?"[2]

Now, Bob was visiting John in the hospital. John had become extremely sick. His doctors finally found the

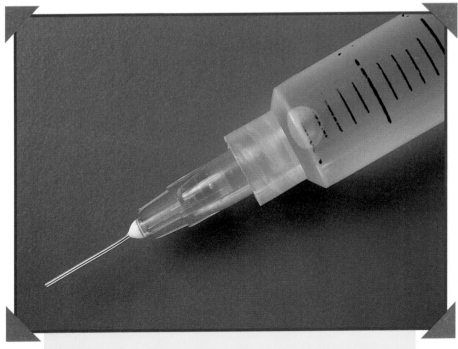

Despite the dangers, John and many other athletes like him often use needles like this one to inject liquid steroids.

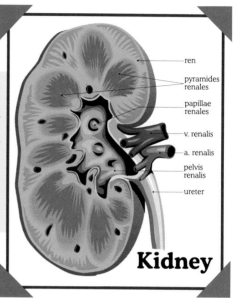

John became extremely sick as a result of steroid use. He developed a rare kidney tumor, and the tumor turned into cancer, which spread to his lungs and other organs.

ren

pyramides
renales

papillae
renales

v. renalis

a. renalis

pelvis
renales

ureter

Kidney

problem—a rare kidney tumor. The tumor soon turned into cancer and spread to his lungs and other organs.

John went through chemotherapy (a series of treatments using very strong chemicals) to try to kill his cancer. The powerful chemicals used in chemotherapy made John nauseous. He vomited a lot. His throat was so irritated that he spit up blood.

In the hospital, Bob was shaken by John's ill health and how he looked. John lost nearly one hundred pounds. All his thick black hair fell out. Even his heavy black eyebrows disappeared. His wrinkled dry skin hung and was ash-green. Bob heard his friend "gasping for air, his voice a hoarse whisper almost unintelligible as he greeted [him] the way he always had."[3]

One day after Bob's visit, John died. Anabolic steroids had caused the rare type of kidney tumor that eventually killed John.

Society and Steroids

Anabolic steroids, usually called steroids, are powerful drugs. They are a form of testosterone, a natural male hormone. (Hormones are the "chemical messengers" in men's and women's bodies. They control such body activities as growth, development, and reproduction.) By taking steroids, a person can create a lean, muscular, strong body quickly. There are significant health risks, however. That is why the use of steroids without a doctor's supervision is against the law.

Steroids Hit the News

Shock roared through the sports world when Canadian sprinter Ben Johnson lost his gold medal at the 1988 Summer Olympic Games. He had broken the old 100-meter dash record. He had even beaten Carl Lewis from the United States.

Lewis finished second, in 9.92 seconds, just .13 of a second behind Ben Johnson.

After the race Ben Johnson tested positive for steroids. He had taken a steroid called stanozolol. When this news was announced, his gold medal was taken away and given to Carl Lewis. The Canadian superstar was further punished by not being allowed to run in international races for two years.

Ben Johnson's disgrace brought international attention to the illegal use of steroids among world-class athletes. The International Olympic Committee had officially banned steroids in 1975. Despite the ban, however, athletes still used them. Other athletic

These people are running for recreation and fun. But sometimes, professional runners take steroids to create a lean, muscular, strong body as a way to win races.

The International Olympic Committee officially banned steroids in 1975.

associations soon followed. At first, athletes were told when they were to be tested, they stopped taking drugs, including steroids. If athletes know when the test will be done, they can stop taking the steroids in time for the drug to get out of the body. So steroid usage among athletes "appeared" to be low.

Then, "surprise" steroid tests were given at some of the 1984 Olympic sporting events. The results? About half the tested athletes had taken steroids. It was not until 1988, though, that the media brought worldwide attention to steroid abuse. For a superstar like Ben Johnson to be stripped of his gold medal because of using steroids was big news.

Today, most major amateur and professional athletic organizations ban steroids. Yet in spite of the many health risks, athletes and nonathletes continue to use them.

Who Takes Steroids—and Why?

Professional and amateur athletes are probably the largest group of steroid users. Many teen athletes try to excel in a sport so they can get a college scholarship. Some teens use steroids to increase their weight, strength, and muscle.

Other people take steroids to boost their confidence or aggressiveness. For example, police officers, firefighters, or construction workers may take steroids to look bigger and tougher. Teens take steroids not just to excel in sports, but also to "perfect" their bodies. Many teens take steroids to help them build muscle fast.

These firefighters are relying on teamwork and experience to put out this blaze. Some people, however, feel they need to take steroids in order to become bigger and stronger. That need for strength and size comes with a dangerous price.

"Tom" (not his real name), a high school student and an athlete, used steroids. He explained why he and other teens were willing to use these drugs. "Kids see the well-built guys on TV getting the girls and the respect from the guys and they want that, too."[1]

Serious weight lifters often go to local gyms. So do teens who are into bodybuilding. There teens meet adults who use steroids to build muscle and bulk up. One teen, age seventeen, said, "Our role model is this older guy, the biggest guy in the gym. . . . He weighs 290 pounds without an ounce of fat . . . that's our goal."[2]

Steroid use is not limited to any one group of teens. Teens from rich, middle-class, and poor families use them. Young people of various races, whether they live in

Teen bodybuilders may resort to steroids as a way to bulk up (get large, rippling muscles) quickly instead of relying on proper dieting and straightforward weight lifting like this teen.

cities, towns, or rural communities, use them. "You see anyone in high school who is big—has ripped mass [large, rippling muscles], the curl in the biceps, the veins—and you know he's on it. He's juiced [taking steroids]," said one teen steroid user.[3]

Males make up the majority of teen users. However, more and more females are using steroids. Their goal is to lose fat and gain muscle. Use of steroids is especially high among teen girls who are into athletic activities such as track and field, soccer, basketball, volleyball, and school dance and drill teams.

No one really knows exactly how many teens use steroids. Because the use of steroids in sports is illegal, it is hard to keep track of exact numbers. One high school coach in Boston told a group of doctors that none of his players took steroids. But one of his players was listening. The teen stood up and told the shocked listeners that seventeen of the coach's top twenty-two athletes were on steroids.[4]

The Numbers—American Teens Who Use Steroids

- More than one million people have used illegal steroids—half are teens.[5]

- Between 5 percent and 12 percent of male high school students and one percent of female students have used steroids by the time they are seniors.[6]

- About three times as many male teens use steroids compared with female teen users.[7]

- More than half the teens who use steroids started

before age sixteen. Some users start as young as age ten.[8]

◆ In a 1992 investigation by *U.S. News and World Report*, 57 percent of teen steroid users said they were influenced to use the drugs by reading muscle magazines. And 42 percent decided to use steroids because they thought famous athletes were taking them.[9]

Cheaters

"Our society continues to greatly reward 'winning at all costs,'" said Dr. Charles Yesalis. Dr. Yesalis is a steroid expert at Pennsylvania State University. Americans emphasize physical appearance over other traits. These negative messages constantly bombard our

Professional weight lifters and other sports players may use steroids in order to become bigger and stronger. However, in the long run they are compromising their health and cheating their competitors out of a fair competition.

young people. The wrong messages are too often being sent that it's OK to cheat to gain a sports advantage and that using chemicals to [change] your body to play sports or to look good is OK.[10]

Steve Courson, a former member of the Pittsburgh Steelers football team agrees.

The root of steroid use is society's addiction to bigger, faster, stronger. The win-at-all-costs mentality [way of thinking] leads to cheating and unethical behavior. I regret few things, but I do regret selling myself out by using drugs to compete.[11]

Courson said that he was introduced to steroids at age eighteen by a college trainer. He used the drugs throughout his college and professional football career. Due to the steroids, he developed serious heart problems.

Courson commented,

In the NFL [National Football League], I was nothing more than a highly paid, highly manipulated gladiator [fighter]. I want kids to know they can be greater than gladiators, that they can use a sport to learn lessons about life and not let the sport use them.[12]

The bottom line: People who use steroids are cheating. Using steroids gives athletes an unfair advantage in sports. Ben Johnson (and the public) will never know whether he won because of his steroid use. Without steroids, he may not have sprinted so fast. People who use steroids to develop their bodies are taking a shortcut. "But really there is no shortcut," according to Arnold Schwarzenegger. He is both an actor and the head of President Clinton's Council on Physical Fitness and Sports.[13]

Booming Black Market

Users often get steroids through illegal and costly means. The heavy demand for steroids has created a black, or illegal, market. Illegal steroid sales top more than $500 million each year.[14]

Some adults who work out in gyms or health clubs or go to various competitions sell the drugs to teens. Sometimes a gym owner sells them. Some doctors and veterinarians write steroid prescriptions for unethical coaches who want teen athletes to bulk up fast. Prescription medications must be bought and used with a doctor's written instructions. However, mail-order

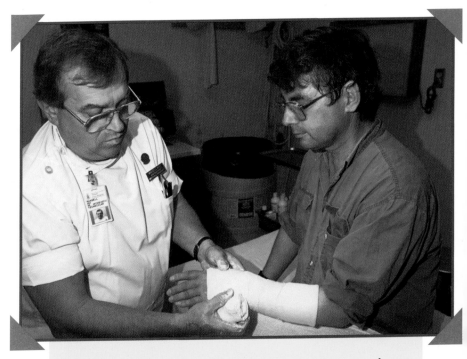

Unlike this doctor who is setting a broken arm, some doctors and veterinarians may write steroid prescriptions for unethical coaches who want their players to bulk up quickly.

sources sell dozens of different steroids. These businesses can send steroids to cities or towns across the United States—without a prescription.

Teens sometimes sell steroids to other teens. According to a 1992 *U.S. News and World Report* article, 25 percent of teens who use steroids say they also sell steroids.[15] In Virginia, one senior high schooler said that he and a friend stole steroids from a drugstore where they both worked. They then sold the stolen drugs at school and made "a killing. Everyone knows you just go to this one guy's locker, and he'll fix you up."[16]

"The challenge of getting hold of the stuff is half the fun," admitted a teen from Iowa. The seventeen-year-old said that he met dealers in parking lots and would taste test the drugs to see whether they were real.[17] What many teens do not know is that from one-third to one-half of the illegal steroids teens buy are fake.[18]

Most black-market steroids are made outside the United States. There is always a chance that they may be fake. Or they may be mixed with other drugs or substances. For example, one teen in Chicago spent thousands of dollars for what he thought were liquid steroids. What he actually got was a mixture of salt and water. Sometimes penicillin, an antibiotic, or veterinary drugs are falsely sold as steroids.

The Law

Both federal and state governments have laws to control anabolic steroids abuse. In 1988, Congress passed the Anti-Drug Abuse Act. This law made distributing and possessing anabolic steroids for nonmedical reasons a federal crime.

In 1990, Congress toughened the laws. Under the

Federal Penalties for Illegal Steroids

Illegal Act	Penalty
First time someone is caught making or distributing steroids	5 years in prison $15,000 fine 2 years mandatory probation
Second time someone is caught making or distributing steroids	10 years in prison $30,000 fine 2 years mandatory probation

Anabolic Steroid Act of 1990, the Drug Enforcement Administration (DEA) regulates, or controls, anabolic steroids. It is a federal crime to nonmedically make, possess, or sell anabolic steroids. If caught, an offender can get up to ten years in prison. This is true in all states and in the District of Columbia.

Look for Signs

Unless you know what to look for, steroid use is sometimes hard to spot. Here are some warning signs:

- Acne or large pimples on face or back
- More intense workouts; interested only in winning
- Problems with law enforcement officials
- Puffy face and body
- Quick weight gain in short periods of time
- Water retention
- Sleeping problems

- ◆ Sudden increase in appetite
- ◆ Sudden mood swings
- ◆ Violent behavior

Steroid abusers also often use jargon or language that is common among other steroid users.

 # Typical Terms of Steroid Users

Term	Meaning
Blending	Mixing different drugs
Buffed	Having large muscles
Bulking up	Increasing muscle mass through steroids
Cycle	The eight-to-twelve-week period when steroids are used. After that, user lets body rest for the same period.
Doping	Using steroids to improve athletic performance
Juice, stuff, or roids	Anabolic steroids
Megadosing	Taking large amounts of steroids
Plateauing	When a steroid no longer works at a certain level
Roid rage	Uncontrolled anger, frustration, or combativeness that results from using anabolic steroids
Roider, juicer, or joy rider	Steroid user who takes the drug only for appearence
Shotgunning	Taking steroids on a hit-or-miss basis
Stacking	Using a combination of steroids
Tapering	Slowly decreasing the use of steroids

Violence and Crime

People on steroids can have wide mood swings. They may feel happy one minute, then suddenly feel angry and bad-tempered the next. Some people become impulsive and exhibit dangerous behavior. Others get depressed and even think about suicide.

Both males and females can become much more aggressive on steroids. This is called roid rage. These bursts of anger can result in violence. No one can predict who will experience roid rage. But roid rage sometimes ends in violence against other people. Acts of violence can lead to arrest and jail time.

The aggressive behavior that comes as a result of steroid use is known as roid rage. Such bursts of rage can sometimes cause violent and dangerous acts of crime where police intervention is necessary.

Darren, an ex-steroid user from Pasadena, California, said he was an "easygoing guy."[19] Then, at age sixteen, he started to use steroids and changed. He remembers, "I was doing everything from being obnoxious to getting out of the car and provoking [starting] fights at intersections. I couldn't handle any kind of stress. I'd just blow!"[20]

"Joe" (not his real name) used steroids and experienced roid rage. "Your whole mentality changes. You go from an intelligent, normal guy to someone who resorts to beating people up if they don't agree with you. It's a totally physical mentality and very aggressive."[21]

In Sharpes, Florida, a mother once again called the police about her son Eric. Then twenty-one, Eric had first started using steroids while in high school. Over the next three years, he was arrested ten times due to his aggressive behavior while on steroids. This time, jail officials put Eric into solitary confinement. That means he was locked in a small cell by himself and could not talk to or see anyone. While in the cell, Eric hanged himself and died.[22] Unfortunately, Eric's violent behavior (a direct result of roid rage) caused other problems for him. No one will ever know exactly why Eric hanged himself. But steroids certainly did not help.

three

Real-Life Stories

During the summer before his senior year in high school, Mike trained hard to be a football star. But the Illinois teen wanted to perform even better. So he started taking steroid pills. Why? "I was playing football and looking for a scholarship. I figured steroids would give me a better chance."[1]

Mike's weight flew up from 147 pounds to 176. However, he never saw his skill as a running back improve much. He stopped using steroids.

Some time later, he tried again. This time, he injected the steroids. He remembered, "I was petrified at first, because I hate needles. But it didn't hurt at all."[2] Again, Mike gained weight and some strength. In the end, though, he lost out on his dream. Because of the extra weight, his tendons loosened in his left shoulder. His shoulder would pop out in every game. He ended up wearing a brace and having operations to repair the damage. His shoulder is now ruined.

Negative Effects Ignored

One teen explained his steroid use this way: "I get side effects [unwanted effects from taking drugs] but I don't mind; it lets me know the stuff is working."[3]

Selling Steroids Is Illegal

In March 1992, a star high school wrestler in New Jersey was caught selling steroids. He was fined. The local newspaper wrote that this was one of "hundreds, perhaps thousands, of cases of steroid use," in central New Jersey schools.[4]

Wasted Time

In a Chicago suburb, Dave planned to go to Daytona Beach, Florida, during his spring break. The high school senior was a weight lifter. He already had a lot of muscle, but he wanted to look better. "I had a friend who was doing Anadrol [a common steroid] that he sold me really cheap," remembered Dave.[5]

He started taking the drug and saw fast results. "My arms were so solid it was unbelievable. I mean they were like bricks."[6] He put on weight and his strength also increased. Dave had a good time during spring break. The week afterward was much different.

Dave explained, "I cut off the 'roids [steroids] a week early, because I didn't want them in my system when I was drinking [in Florida]. But it didn't work. Flying home on the plane, I was so sick I thought I was going to die."[7] Not only was Dave sick, his body changed. After he stopped using steroids, his weight and strength gains disappeared. He said, "I ended up smaller and weaker than I was before. It was a waste of time."[8]

Teen Takes Own Life

An eighteen-year-old decided to increase his size and strength, so he bought and used anabolic steroids illegally. The young man's father told his son several times to stop using them. However, neither father nor son knew about the changes that steroids can cause. Depression is fairly common once a teen stops using the drugs.

Finally, the young man listened to his father, and stopped using the steroids. But he soon became extremely depressed. One month later, he killed himself. He didn't leave a note, so no one will ever know exactly what drove this young man to such a drastic act. But the depression brought on by steroid withdrawal certainly did not help.

Justly Rewarded?

Brian Bosworth, a former professional football player with the Seattle Seahawks, tested positive for steroid use during his days as a linebacker for the University of Oklahoma. Nonetheless, Bosworth's contract with the Seahawks for ten years, $11 million, was the largest National Football League rookie contract at that time (1987). Bosworth played only twenty-five games for the Seattle Seahawks before a shoulder injury forced him to retire from football. He has since stopped using steroids and hopes for a successful Hollywood movie career.

Hogan's Phony Muscles

Professional wrestler Hulk Hogan stands six feet six inches tall and weighs just under three hundred pounds. Every year, he earns millions of dollars for doing commercials and movies. He has also won the World Wrestling

Federation championship several times. Since the late 1970s, the superstar has said that he does not use steroids. "I am not a steroid abuser. It's like putting poison in your body," he said on a TV talk show in 1991.[9] He did admit that he had used steroids for a short time in 1983. But he said that a doctor had prescribed the drugs for torn biceps.

Then in July 1994, Hogan had to go to court. He had to testify in a steroid case against Vincent McMahon, owner of the World Wrestling Foundation. That is when he confessed that he had used steroids to "get big."[10] He also said that McMahon helped make the steroids available. "I would go by the office and pick up the

These amateur wrestlers are simply enjoying the sport and the natural strength and agility it requires. Unfortunately, some professional athletes seek a competitive edge by using steroids.

steroids along with my paycheck and fan mail," Hogan explained.[11]

During the case against McMahon, Hogan said about 80 percent—that is, four out of every five—wrestlers that he knew in the 1980s used steroids.

Risk Taker

After "Tom" (not his real name) broke his leg, he began weight training to keep fit. His body firmed up and his muscles got bigger. But, he said, "I wanted more size, faster."[12] A training partner suggested steroids. So, for a summer, Tom used steroids. He took steroid pills and also injected the drug into the muscles of his buttocks. Back in school in September, he was surprised. "I got a huge response, from guys and girls. I was sort of shocked at first, but after a while, I began to like it."[13]

When Tom stopped using steroids, he quickly lost weight. He bought more steroids and began using them again. He explained, "You might be able to dodge the physical side-effects for a long time if you know what you're doing. But you can't avoid what steroids do to your head."[14] (Roid rage is an all-too-common side effect.)

Parent Pushers

Sometimes parents push their teens into taking steroids. Philip Halpern, a San Diego lawyer, said, "I've uncovered numerous examples of fathers getting steroids for their kids because they wanted them to be better athletes."[15]

One tenth grader hoped to play professional football in the future. "My stepdad says he's going to start me up on steroids as soon as I'm done growing," said the teen.[16]

Pushing at the Gym

Greg started working out in a local gym. That is where he bought his first steroids. At first, the drugs worked for him. In a little less than twenty-two months, he went from 183 pounds to 242 pounds. He developed lots of muscle. Pleased with the result, he used steroids for thirteen years. Then, he began selling steroids to teens. Over the years, he estimated that he had sold steroids to more than one hundred teens. He remembered, "I had this one kid, fifteen years old—I made a monster out of him. I took him from 150 pounds to 236 in a year, and he was out of control, fighting, stealing."[17]

As a result of his own steroid use, Greg developed

Working out at a gym or health club is a good way to stay in shape, but steroids are never a necessary part of an exercise routine. The side effects that come with steroid abuse can be life threatening in some cases.

high blood pressure and swollen lymph nodes. (Lymph nodes contain large cells that absorb harmful matter and dead tissue. They are bunched together in the neck, armpits, groin, and near other organs and large blood vessels.) Greg also grew to feel guilty about what he had done to the young people he had sold steroids to.

He turned his life around and now talks to young people in schools about the dangers of steroids.

four

Dangers of Steroids

European researchers first developed steroids in the 1930s. Their goal was to help people rebuild body tissue that had broken down from disease. After World War II ended in 1945, steroids had a new use. They were given to the many starving people found in concentration camps. These drugs helped the skeletal prisoners build up their body weight.

Use of steroids in sports began in the early 1950s. During the Olympic Games, the athletic community discovered that some Soviet and Eastern European athletes had taken large amounts of steroids. As a result, they had big muscles and great strength. When this news traveled around the world, athletes in other countries began to use steroids.

Steroids can cause many dangerous side effects. They also give an unfair advantage to the athletes who use them. That unfair advantage is why steroids have been outlawed in the Olympics since 1975. Most amateur and professional sports organizations also ban and test for steroids regularly.

Steroids Defined

Anabolic steroids are compounds that resemble testosterone, the male sex hormone. They are synthetic, which means they are made in laboratories. Hundreds of different steroids have been synthesized. Each one has different effects. Some steroids are used to treat illness or injury. Other forms of steroids build strength and muscles.

Although testosterone is called a male hormone, it is found in both males and females. But males produce much more testosterone than females.

The adult male, on the average, naturally makes from 2.5 to 11 milligrams (mg) of testosterone each day. In contrast, the average steroid user takes more than 100 mg a day.[1]

Sports Organizations That Ban Steroids

- International Amateur Athletic Federation

- International Federation of Bodybuilders

- International Olympic Committee

- National Collegiate Athletic Association

- National Football League

Functions of Testosterone

♦ Can influence emotions

♦ Causes skin and hair to grow

♦ Helps build bone and muscle

♦ Maintains the sexual organs

♦ Once a boy starts to mature, testosterone causes his body hair to grow and his voice to deepen.

Anabolic steroids can be taken in tablet or liquid form. The liquid form is injected into muscle. Most injected anabolic steroids are stored in the body's fat. They remain there for several weeks. As long as they are in the body, they can cause health problems.

Medical Uses

Some steroids are helpful medical drugs—when taken properly under the supervision of a doctor. The corticosteroid called cortisone is an example of a useful steroid. Cortisone is used to treat a range of health problems, from tendon injuries to vision problems.

Doctors must use steroids carefully and in small amounts because steroids can produce many side effects. It is the nonmedical, illegal use of steroids that is of concern. The amount taken illegally by an adult or teen is often fifty to one hundred times the amount used by doctors to treat diseases. Such excess can cause many

Certain Steroids Can Help Treat:

- Allergic skin rashs.

- Androgen-deficiency disease. Men with this disease cannot make enough of their own testosterone.

- Blood diseases such as anemia and kidney failure. (Anemia occurs when the body does not produce enough red blood cells.)

- Lack of muscle production. Sometimes people with certain forms of cancer, burns, and AIDS can be helped with steroids.

- Osteoporosis, or thinning of the bones.

- Some breast cancers.

health problems. Sometimes, taking too much steroid can cause death, as happened to one young man. Complaining of severe pain, a twenty-three-year-old bodybuilder was taken to the hospital. Doctors found that his liver and kidneys had stopped working. He was rushed to the intensive-care unit. But four days later, his heart stopped and he died. When doctors examined his body again, they discovered high levels of steroids.[2]

Do Steroids Work?

Anabolic steroids mimic the bodybuilding effects of testosterone. So anabolic steroids do cause muscles to grow. Athletes who have used these drugs report an increase in muscle mass, strength, and endurance. People gain weight on steroids. Often, though, the weight gain is a result of water retention.

These changes are not permanent. People who take steroids illegally often megadose. They take huge amounts each day. Most cycle their steroid use. They take the drug for several days, stop taking it for several days, then continue this on-off cycle. Others take steroids for six to twelve weeks or more, stop for several weeks, then start another megadose cycle. During the time people are off steroids, they lose weight and strength.

Richard L. Sandlin is a former assistant coach with the University of Alabama. He said,

> I took steroids from 1976 to 1983. In the middle of 1979, my body began turning a yellowish color. I was very aggressive and combative, had high blood pressure and testicular atrophy [shrinking of the testes]. I was hospitalized twice with near kidney failure, liver tumors, and severe personality disorders [changes]. During my second hospital stay, the doctors found I had become sterile. Two years after I quit using and started training without drugs, I set six new world records in power lifting, something I thought was impossible without the steroids.[3]

The Dangers

Some of steroids' effects, such as rapid weight gain and muscle mass, are easy to see. Some changes take place inside the body and may not be seen until it is too late. Some effects are not reversible. Here is a rundown of the dangers of steroids.

One former bodybuilder remembered this about what steroids did to a friend:

This woman friend of mine walked into the gym after being gone for three weeks. Her face was square and had unusual amounts of blond hair all over it. Her voice was really deep and her back had acne on it which she never had before. She went from beauty to freak in three weeks.[4]

His friend had been injecting large doses of steroids.

Continued use of steroids can cause many health problems in both men and women.

Aaron began using steroids when he was a teen. He was a bodybuilder and worked out regularly. He wanted to be bigger and stronger. "In basically three to six months I went from being able to bench press 250 pounds once, and it was difficult doing it once, to doing 12 reps (repetitions) with 300 pounds easily."[5] But he

Steroid-Causing Problems in Males

- Acne
- Baldness or hair loss
- Depression
- High-pitched voice
- Inability to get an erection
- Increased or decreased sex drive
- Increased risk of testicle or prostate cancer
- Infertility (inability to reproduce)
- Large breasts
- Low sperm count
- Pain when urinating
- Shrinking of the testicles (Testicles are the male sex glands that produce sperm.)
- Sleeping problems

Steroid-Causing Problems in Females

- Acne
- Baldness, irreversible
- Changes in or stopping of menstrual cycles
- Deepened voice
- Hair on the face
- Increased or decreased sex drive
- Infertility (inability to reproduce)
- Shrinking breasts

developed serious liver problems from using steroids. He nearly died.

Aaron now says that steroids are too risky. "I'm here to tell people and especially young people that yes, it can happen, and yes, it will happen to you."[6]

Benji was not as lucky as Aaron. Benji was a seventeen-year-old high school senior who played football for Ashtabula High School in Ohio. During practice on Halloween, he collapsed. He died in a nearby hospital. What killed him? Steroids, said the doctors. They found that his heart was diseased, his testicles had shrunk, and he had puncture wounds on his thighs. Friends said that Benji wanted to be "big" and that the teen believed that "steroids were not harming him or that taking them was worth the risk."[7]

Other Dangers

There are other serious dangers associated with using steroids. Most people who begin using steroids take them as pills. Some then decide to use syringes and needles to

Steroid-Causing Problems in Males and Females

- Aching joints
- Acne
- Addiction
- Bad breath
- Chills
- Constant headaches
- Death
- Feeling tired
- Fever
- Heart disease
- High blood pressure
- Hives
- Inability to stop the growth of cancer cells
- Increased likelihood of injuring muscles and joints; longer time to heal from injury when on steroids.
- Increased risk of heart attack or stroke
- Kidney disease
- Liver damage and cancers
- Muscle cramps
- Rashs
- Roid rage
- Sore tongue
- Stomach pain
- Swelling of feet or ankles
- Trembling
- Vomiting of blood
- Yellow skin or eyes

inject the steroids. Many brands of steroids must be injected with huge syringes and large, 1.5-inch needles. "The first time I tried to inject myself, I almost fainted, and one of my friends did faint," said one nineteen-year-old from Arizona. "Sometimes one of the guys will inject in one side of his butt one day and the other the next. Then, we all laugh at him because he can barely sit down for the next three days."[8]

One weight lifter said, "We all knew who was using. We exchanged information on any new drugs that were on the market. We got our steroids through the gym owner. In fact, he would inject them for us, in the rear."[9]

If needles are shared, steroid users can get dangerous infections, such as hepatitis or the HIV infection.

Also, because most people buy steroids illegally, they really do not know exactly what they are buying. A user could be taking drugs other than steroids and not know it.

Teen Alert

If children or teens use steroids, it can prevent their bones from growing properly. That means they will not grow to their full height. Even small doses of steroids can affect height permanently. That is why doctors seldom prescribe anabolic steroids for children or teens.

Anabolic steroids also make the tendons weak. Tendons connect muscles to bones. Weakened tendons cannot carry the extra weight that users put on and can tear or break down.

Personality Changes

People taking steroids can find that the drugs cause unpredictable mood and personality changes. The user may become angry or hostile over small things. Users can also fly into sudden rages.

Steroid's Hook

People on steroids can grow addicted to them. When this happens, steroid users crave or strongly desire the drug and have a hard time stopping its use. They cannot control their use of steroids and become dependent on them.

When users who are dependent on steroids stop using them, they go through withdrawal. Withdrawal is

Steroid-Causing Personality Changes

- ◆ Depression
- ◆ Impulsive behavior
- ◆ Increased aggressiveness
- ◆ Irritability

- ◆ Jealousy
- ◆ Temper tantrums
- ◆ Unusual moods and behaviors

the process of ridding the body of a drug. Withdrawal can produce many symptoms. Many former steroid users tell of suicide attempts.[10]

"I tend to get really depressed when I go off a cycle," said a Maryland teen. "On a bad day, I think 'Gee, if I were on the stuff this wouldn't be happening.'"[11]

Lyle Alzado's Story

Although Lyle Alzado was fast, he was not big enough for professional football. So, in 1969, while in college, he began taking steroids. He found them easy to get. By using steroids, eating a lot, and working out, he soon went from 190 pounds to about 300 pounds. Two years later, he played defensive end with the Denver Broncos. Alzado kept taking steroids. He said:

> I kept on because I knew I had to keep getting more size. I became very violent on the field. Off it, too. I did things only crazy people do. Once in 1979 in Denver a guy sideswiped my car, and I chased him up and down hills through the neighborhoods. I did that a lot. I'd chase a guy, pull him out of his car, and beat . . . him.[12]

Later, Alzado played with the Cleveland Browns and Los Angeles Raiders. Twice during his career he made All-Pro. No matter which professional football team he joined, he continued to take steroids. He also helped other football players get steroids if he was asked.

Alzado admitted, "I was so wild about winning. It's all I cared about, winning, winning, winning. . . . I felt I had to keep up. I didn't sleep much, maybe three or four hours a night. My system would run so fast."[13]

He explained why he could not stop. "It was addicting, mentally addicting. I just didn't feel strong unless I was taking something."[14]

Alzado knew the drugs were not good for him. His cholesterol level skyrocketed to more than four hundred. (Anything higher than 250 is considered a potential problem.) From injecting so many steroids into his buttocks, he had to have lumps of hard tissue removed. Some of the lumps were larger than baseballs. He remembered, "I got moodier and moodier, too. I had a couple of divorces. I yelled all the time. Anytime I'd walk into a restaurant or bar, I always felt like I had to check

Withdrawal Symptoms

- Depression
- Headache
- Inability to sleep
- Loss of energy and appetite
- Muscle shrinkage
- Nausea
- Sweating
- Weight loss

everything out to make sure no one was going to mess with me."[15]

Even after Alzado retired from the NFL in 1985, he kept taking steroids. "I couldn't stand the thought of being weak. I tried to taper down."[16] He also tried a comeback with the Raiders in 1990, but he hurt his knee. After knee surgery, he was cut from the team. Soon after, he fainted. When he came to, blood was pouring down his face. He had broken his nose and needed surgery.

After four days in the hospital, Alzado went home. But he noticed he would feel dizzy sometimes. He had trouble with his balance and coordination. He tilted to the right when he walked. When he started seeing double and slurring his speech, he went back into the hospital. There he was told he had incurable brain cancer.

Alzado believed that his use of steroids caused his cancer. One of the doctors who treated him agreed. In fact, the doctor kept warning Alzado to stop taking steroids. After his cancer was found, Alzado said,

> If I had known that I would be this sick now, I would have tried to make it in football on my own—naturally. Whoever is doing this stuff, if you stay on it too long or maybe if you get on it at all, you're going to get something bad from it. I don't mean you'll definitely get brain cancer, but you'll get something. It is a wrong thing to do.[17]

Alzado told his story to *Sports Illustrated* magazine in July 1991. One year later, he was dead. His final words in the *Sports Illustrated* article were "My strength isn't my strength anymore. My strength is my heart. If you're on steroids or human growth hormone [a steroid substitute], stop. I should have."[18]

five

Fighting Steroid Abuse

Two important factors in combating steroid abuse are awareness and education. Federal drug programs, schools, communities, and individuals provide information, education, and help in dealing with steroids.

Orange County Colleges

Several colleges in Orange County, California, have developed programs on steroid abuse. Some of their material focuses on the negative effects of steroid use. The colleges also have written policies to explain why athletes should not use anabolic steroids. The policies tell student athletes that these colleges accept only fair sports events. Using steroids is cheating. Athletes can be tested for steroids at any time. If they are found to be users, colleges will get them treatment help.

ATLAS Program

One drug program called ATLAS (Adolescents Training and Learning to Avoid Steroids) has proven to be a success. ATLAS was created by scientists at the Oregon Health Sciences University. This prevention and education program teaches teens about anabolic steroids and how to avoid taking them. The study ran for one year in thirty-one schools in Portland, Oregon. A total of 1,506 football players and students went through ATLAS during the football season.

The program is team-based. Coaches and student team leaders give seven weekly, fifty-minute classes on a variety of topics: effects of steroids, sports nutrition, strength training, drug refusal, and antisteroid media messages. In addition, seven weight-room sessions are

Drug programs such as ATLAS teach teens about the risks associated with taking steroids and how to avoid them.

taught by Oregon Health Sciences University research staff. Parents are given information on ATLAS and are invited to a discussion meeting.

"ATLAS is a very unique approach to dealing with the problem of steroid use among athletes," said Dr. Linn Goldberg, head of the ATLAS program. "It involves a team-approach that empowers student athletes to make the right choices through education. And we now know it works."[1]

Minnesota State High School League

The state of Minnesota ran an eight-to-ten-week training program for students, coaches, and trainers. An important part of the program was drug education. Steroids were covered because it is "really a serious issue," said Dorothy E. McIntyre, associate executive director of the Minnesota State High School League.[2] This organization produced a video on steroids that was used in schools around the state.

Federal Government

Three federal agencies—National Clearinghouse for Alcohol and Drug Abuse Information, United States Department of Education, and National Institute of Drug Abuse—publish a variety of information on steroids. Their booklets, pamphlets, and books are available by mail or through their sites on the World Wide Web.

Communities

Various national groups and local communities are working to combat steroid use.

Medical Organizations

The American Medical Association (AMA) condemns or strongly disapproves the use of steroids by athletes. Other medical associations agree with the AMA, including the American Academy of Pediatrics, American College of Sports Medicine, American Academy of Orthopedic Surgeons, and American Osteopathic Academy of Sports Medicine. Several of these organizations have put together brochures on the dangers of steroids.

TARGET Program

The National Federation of State High School Associations is headquartered in Kansas City, Missouri. It supports after-school athletic, music, speech, and debate programs in more than twenty thousand high schools in the United States and Canada. Its TARGET Program provides information about drugs, including steroids. Much of the program is aimed at coaches of teen athletes. TARGET explains to coaches the warning signs of steroid use and what to do if someone may be on steroids. It also recommends a plan to keep steroids away from athletes and schools.

National Steroid Research Center (NSRC)

John L. Lestini, Jr., is a big fan of the Pittsburgh Steelers. Lestini came to know former Steeler football player Steve Courson. Courson had used steroids during college and in his early football career. Now he had serious heart problems from the steroids. To warn others about the dangers of steroids, Courson gave talks to adults and teens. Lestini began to go with Courson. "I gained enormous knowledge on steroids by just sitting back and listening to Steve talk to groups around the country," Lestini said.[3]

Then in 1989, Lestini founded the National Steroid Research Center and Other Drugs of Abuse in Sports. "This all came about when Mike Webster and a couple other former Steeler players approached me about helping one of their teammates who had used steroids and was very ill," remembered Lestini.[4] The National Steroid Research Center is in downtown Weirton, West Virginia. John L. Lestini, Jr., is the chair and director.

So far, the NSRC has accomplished the following:

- ◆ Its staff members have spoken on television and radio talk shows, at colleges, at public schools, and at hospitals, as well as with the police throughout the United States.

- ◆ It helped with the passage of the Anabolic Steroid Act of 1990. (This law makes selling steroids a federal crime. Selling steroids can carry up to a five-year prison sentence and large fines. Simply using steroids could bring the user large fines and time in prison as well.)

- ◆ It offers a variety of materials and referrals on steroids to kids, teens, teachers, coaches, professional groups, health professionals, and law enforcement personnel.

- ◆ It runs an 800-number telephone steroid hot line. NSRC gets calls from around the United States. A typical one: "My son is becoming so aggressive. He's gained thirty to fifty pounds in the last four months. He's losing concern for everything except athletic training."[5]

"Steroid abuse is a family problem," Lestini said. "The

A strong family like this one can help if a family member has a problem to overcome.

emotional changes affect every member of the family involved."[6]

Individuals

Just one person can make a big difference in the fight against illegal steroid use.

Greg Kostas

While working out at a local gym, Greg Kostas started using steroids. As time went on, he sold steroids to teens at the same gym. He did this for thirteen years. Today, Kostas still works out. But he stopped taking steroids years ago. From all his steroid use, he developed serious health problems such as high blood pressure and swollen lymph nodes. And he felt guilty about turning teens on to steroids. "I did wrong for thirteen years, and it was time to set it right." He now talks to teens at the same local gym about the hazards of steroids.[7]

Brian Isetts

Brian Isetts, a pharmacist, has talked to thousands of teens about the dangers of steroids. Isetts is an instructor in the Pharmaceutical Care Laboratory at the University of Minnesota, College of Pharmacy. He is also director of professional affairs for the Minnesota Pharmacists Association. He estimates that from 3 to 4 percent of all high-school-age male teens have used steroids. He has also noted that "often teens on steroids also have a problem with alcohol."[8]

Isetts is part of a network of pharmacists that focuses on steroid education in schools. About fifteen to twenty other pharmacists participate in this nationwide program. Isetts begins his discussion by talking about the current attitude that "Winning is everything in America. There are a lot of pressures on young people today. I think we've lost sight of what sports is all about. Nowadays, it's high stake games with lots of money."[9]

He goes over the effects of steroids. "Guys are uncomfortable when they hear that their testicles can shrink or their breasts can grow. Steroids jeopardize their health. My goal is to give accurate information so they can make informed choices."[10]

Isetts sometimes brings in guest speakers—former steroid users who have ruined their health by taking steroids. Isetts encourages teens to ask questions and share their concerns.[11]

six

What You Can Do

Peer pressure and winning are reasons that teens give for using steroids. Teens want to be liked and accepted by others. But only they can decide what to put into their bodies—and they can encourage others to stay away from steroids and other drugs.

Saying No to Steroids

It is not always easy to say no. Saying no to steroids and other drugs takes courage. However, by refusing to use steroids or take drugs, teens show they value themselves. They are also saying that they are responsible for what they do and decide not to do.

Quitting

If you or someone you know wants to quit using steroids or other drugs, call or write

- Alateen, a organization of Al-Anon. Alateen is for teen friends and family members of drug abusers. It has chapters in cities across the United States.

- Drug treatment programs or chemical dependency programs

- Family or friends

- Hot lines and referral services

- Mental health agencies

- Organizations in your area. (Look in the telephone book's yellow pages under "Community Services" or "Drug Abuse.")

- Teachers, school counselors, drug abuse counselors, your physician, or other health professionals

Tell Others About Steroid Abuse

To help get information out about the dangers of steroid abuse, here are some steps to take:

- Ask local businesses, such as the gas or telephone company, to include bill stuffers about the dangers of steroid abuse.

- Create fact sheets about steroid abuse. Include telephone numbers of places that people can call for help or for more information. Ask local supermarkets if they will stuff your fact sheet in customers' bags.

- Create posters that warn about steroid abuse. Include telephone numbers of organizations people can call for help or for more information. Ask the owners or managers of places that kids and teens often go to if you can put up your posters. Try recreation centers, music stores, fast-food restaurants, pizza places, ice-cream parlors, candy stores, movie theaters, supermarkets, and youth centers.

♦ Write a letter about steroid abuse to the editor of your community and local newspapers.

Enjoy Drug-Free Fun

Looking good and feeling good are great reasons to avoid using steroids and other drugs. Millions of kids and teens across the United States stay free of steroids and other harmful substances. They know that using drugs does not solve problems or add anything to their lives.

There are lots of ways to enjoy life. For example, learning a new skill can be fun. Taking lessons will help build skill and confidence. Debate, karate lessons, skating, rollerblading, water or snow skiing, skateboarding, or trying out for a play are all good alternatives to drug use. Sports such as tennis, volleyball, soccer, basketball, baseball, hockey, and track also provide fun, healthy outlets.

Volunteering is also rewarding and fun. Volunteer work is often available at hospitals, day care centers, food banks, nature centers, or nursing homes. Volunteers also teach people to read or read for people who have trouble seeing.

Putting together a neighborhood newspaper is a great way to keep your neighbors current on what is happening. Sophia Williard, age nine, of Mount Lebanon, Pennsylvania, had a lemonade stand at the end of her driveway. She got to know a lot of the neighbors this way. But, "I got bored with that, but I still wanted to make money and help people get to know one another."[1]

So, in 1996, she started a neighborhood paper. A year later, she had forty paying subscribers. She puts out six issues a year. Her papers include local news, sports, comics, poetry, trivia, surveys, and ads.

Michael Attardo, Jr., age eleven, explained his money-making idea. "I had this idea where kids can bring in their stuff and sell it and probably makes some money."[2] Michael's idea became Kid Biz. It is an outdoor marketplace in Buffalo, New York, run by young people, between the ages of seven and eleven. In the first year, more than forty young people completed a training class. They then each paid two dollars to rent a booth in a local park for one Saturday each month. Every Saturday, each young person made between ten and seventy dollars. They sold snow cones, cotton candy, painted rocks, jewelry, designer pencils, used books, toys, and lemonade.

Peer support groups at schools can help kids discuss and deal with daily life issues and decisions. They also offer fun activities and sometimes increase cultural awareness. After-school programs or groups such as Boys and Girls Clubs of America, Boy Scouts, and Girl Scouts may offer programs like this. Belonging to groups like these is a great way to meet new friends and do exciting activities.

Peer leadership programs and peer counseling interventions at your school or community center are another way to meet and help people. These programs help young people learn how to speak before an audience, organize tasks, talk with peers and adults, and run group meetings. Peer leaders sometimes speak at conferences and meetings or co-lead drug-prevention activities. Peer-counseling interventions involve young people who help their peers through one-on-one sessions, informal street talks, or answering a telephone hot line.

The Keys

It takes hard work and time to develop and train the body. And it takes much more than muscles or strength to be a star athlete. Athletic ability depends on strength, endurance, skill, and mental keenness. It also depends on diet, rest, natural ability, and overall mental and physical health. Athletic excellence is achieved by millions without using dangerous steroids and other drugs.

Training

Coaches help athletes train for particular sports. Finding the right balance for training is essential. Overtraining can lead to fatigue and injuries. Coaches know that a mix of aerobic exercise, strength training, exercise drills, and rest is best.

Proper training is an essential element in any sport. With the proper physical and mental conditioning, sports can be a fun and rewarding experience.

They also can help with mental conditioning. Many coaches use four methods: positive imagery, goal setting, relaxation training, and assertiveness training.

Positive Imagery. This method combines deep breathing and visualizing an upcoming athletic event. In your mind, you "see" yourself crossing the finish line or shooting a successful free throw.

Goal Setting. First, goals are identified, then the steps needed to reach those goals are laid out. The athlete goes through the steps, one at a time, getting closer and closer to the goals. When a goal is achieved, a new one is set.

Relaxation Training. This method teaches muscle relaxation and helps concentration.

Assertiveness Training. This method deals with controlling anger, thinking positively, and coping with disapproval and fear.

Mel's Story

Mel took swimming lessons at age three at the local YMCA. As he got older, he won many swimming races.

> I didn't grow at all between age twelve and thirteen, at a time when some of my competitors grew five inches. I didn't win for a year while I waited for that growth spurt—and it was pretty hard to swallow. But fortunately, I had great parents and a great coach who told me that swimming was about improvement, not about winning. Being talented is only part of the equation for an athlete. You need determination, you need a good coach, you need your family behind you, you need your own feelings of self-worth and security—and then some luck, too. And I had all the ingredients.[3]

Mel continued to swim. He also studied hard and was an honor student. The talented athlete went to his first

Swimming is a fun, healthful way to exercise. With hard work and proper training, one can have fun and win competitions.

Olympics in 1988. But he did not win a medal. He remembered, "I was so in awe, and so gripped by fear. The fear paralyzed me."[4]

He still believed in himself. He did not turn to steroids or other drugs. Instead, he set new goals for himself. "I said that I would make 'baby step' improvements every day, and that in four years I would go into the next [Olympic] Games."[5] Mel kept his promise to himself. At the 1992 Olympic Summer Games at Barcelona, Spain, he put all his physical and mental training to work. The results: He won two gold swimming medals and set a new world record in the 200-meter butterfly.

The swimming champion told teens, "If it's a challenge, race toward it, don't shy away. You can't have any other attitude toward life."[6]

questions for discussion

1. It is often hard for someone with a steroid problem to get help. Why do you think this is true?

2. If you think that one of your friends has used steroids, what would you do?

3. What would you do if you found out that a friend was selling steroids?

4. How many kids do you know who have used or are using steroids? How do you feel about their steroid use?

5. If someone wants you to try steroids, what are some refusals you would feel comfortable using? Have you practiced saying them?

6. Has anyone approached you about using steroids? If yes, how did you handle it? Now that you have read this book, would you have done or said something different?

7. If someone sells steroids to teens, should that person receive a tougher penalty than someone who sells to adults?

8. What do you like to do to get a natural high? Many kids like to swim. Some like to play basketball, baseball, soccer, or tennis. Some like to skate, write, draw, or paint.

9. In what other ways could your community educate people about steroids?

10. Do you think all schools should have drug information programs for their athletes? Explain your answer.

chapter notes

Chapter 1. John's Story

1. Bob Goldman and Ronald Klatz, *Death in the Locker Room: Drugs & Sports* (Chicago: Elite Sports Medicine Publications, Inc., 1992), p. 3.

2. Ibid., p. 2.

3. Ibid.

Chapter 2. Society and Steroids

1. James Deacon, "Biceps in a Bottle," *Maclean's*, May 2, 1994, p. 52.

2. Joannie M. Schrof, "Pumped Up," *U.S. News & World Report*, June 1, 1992, p. 61.

3. Deacon, p. 52.

4. Skip Rozin, "Steroids and Sports: What Price Glory?" *Business Week*, October 17, 1994, p. 177.

5. "Anabolic Steroid Use Rising Among Teenage Girls; Stable Among Boys," press release, Penn State University, December 15, 1997 <http://www.psu.edu/ur/NEWS/girlsteroid.html/>.

6. Drug Enforcement Administration, *Drugs of Abuse* (Arlington, Va.: U.S. Department of Justice, 1996), p. 40.

7. Robert Mathias, "Steroid Prevention Program Scores with High School Athletes," *NIDA Notes*, July/August 1997, p. 15.

8. Schrof, p. 55.

9. Ibid.

10. "Anabolic Steroid Use Rising Among Teenage Girls; Stable Among Boys," <http://www.psu.edu/ur/>.

11. Schrof, p. 61.

12. Ibid., pp. 62–63.

13. Kenneth T. Walsh, "Schwarzenegger Speaks: Steroids Don't Pay Off," *U.S. News & World Report*, June 1, 1992, p. 63.

14. Darryl S. Inaba, William E. Cohen, and Michael E. Holstein, *Uppers, Downers, All Arounders: Physical and Mental Effects of Psychoactive Drugs* (Ashland, Oreg.: CNS Publications, Inc., 1997), p. 273.

15. Schrof, p. 61.

16. Ibid.

17. Ibid.

18. Ibid.

19. "Hooked," *The Chemical People Newsletter*, September/October 1992, p. 2.

20. Ibid.

21. Deacon, p. 52.

22. Lynne Bumpus-Hooper, "Brevard Parents Sue Over Son's Suicide in Jail," *The Orlando Sentinel*, October 13, 1995, pp. D-1, D-4.

Chapter 3. Real-Life Stories

1. Frank Kuznik, "The Steroid Epidemic," *Boston Sunday Herald*, May 15–17, 1992, p. 4.

2. Ibid., p. 5.

3. Joannie M. Schrof, "Pumped Up," *U.S. News & World Report*, June 1, 1992, p. 56.

4. Kuznik, p. 4.

5. Ibid.

6. Ibid., p. 5.

7. Ibid.

8. Ibid.

9. Michael A. Lipton, "Incredible Hulk?" *People*, March 23, 1992, p. 91.

10. "House of Mirrors Lures Body Builders into Steroid Abuse," SIUC News, press release, Southern Illinois University of Carbondale, University News Service, July 29, 1994, p. 3.

11. Ibid.

12. James Deacon, "Biceps in a Bottle," *Maclean's*, May 2, 1994, p. 52.

13. Ibid.

14. Ibid.

15. Fultz, Oliver, "'Roid Rage," *American Health*, May 1991, pp. 60–66.

16. Schrof, p. 61.

17. Skip Rozin, "Steroids: A Spreading Peril," *Business Week*, June 19, 1995, p. 139.

Chapter 4. Dangers of Steroids

1. Raja Mishra, "Steroids and Sports Are a Losing Combination," Rockville, Md.: Food and Drug Administration, 1997, <http://www.medaccess.com/consumer_rep/hc0042. htm>.

2. Ibid.

3. Darryl S. Inaba, William E. Cohen, and Michael E. Holstein, *Uppers, Downers, All Arounders: Physical and Mental Effects of Psychoactive Drugs* (Ashland, Oreg.: CNS Publications, Inc., 1997), p. 271.

4. Ibid., p. 270.

5. "Steroid Abuse," WRAL OnLine, <http//www.wral.tv. com/features/healthteam/1996/0722-steroids/>.

6. Ibid.

7. Rick Telander and Merrell Noden, "The Death of an Athlete," *Sports Illustrated*, February 20, 1989, pp. 68–72.

8. Joannie M. Schrof, "Pumped Up," *U.S. News & World Report*, June 1, 1992, p. 61.

9. Inaba, Cohen, and Holstein, pp. 271–272.

10. Center for Substance Abuse Prevention, *If You Use Steroids, These Aren't the Only Things Stacked Against You* (Rockville, Md.: Substance Abuse and Mental Health Administration, 1993).

11. Schrof, p. 59.

12. Lyle Alzado, "I'm Sick and I'm Scared," *Sports Illustrated*, July 8, 1991, pp. 20–24.

13. Ibid.

14. Ibid.

15. Ibid.

16. Ibid.

17. Ibid.

18. Ibid.

Chapter 5. Fighting Steroid Abuse

1. National Institutes of Health, "New Drug Prevention Program Helps Student Athletes Avoid Steroids Use," press release, National Institute on Drug Abuse, November 19, 1996. <http://www.nih.gov/news/pr/ nov96/nida-19.htm>.

2. Author interview with Dorothy E. McIntyre, May 20, 1997.

3. Kim North, "Lestini Fighting Steroids," *The Intelligencer*, February 1, 1995, p. 11.

4. Ibid.

5. Letter to author from John Lestini, December 8, 1995.

6. North, p. 11.

7. Skip Rozin, "Steroids: A Spreading Peril," *Business Week*, June 19, 1995, p. 139.

8. Author interview with Brian Isetts, June 17, 1997.

9. Ibid.

10. Ibid.

11. Ibid.

Chapter 6. What You Can Do

1. Deborah J Baer, "From Whiz Kids to Biz Kids," *Ladies' Home Journal*, July 1997, p. 60.

2. Ibid.

3. Mel Stewart, "Going for the Gold (Again)," *Current Health 2*, May 1996, p. 11.

4. Ibid.

5. Ibid.

6. Ibid.

where to write

Alateen
P.O. Box 862
Midtown Station
New York, NY 10018-0862
(212) 302-7240
<http://www.al-anon.org>

American Council for Drug Education
136 East 64th Street
New York, NY 10021
(212) 758-8060

Drug Enforcement Administration
Demand Reduction Section
Washington, DC 20537
(202) 307-7936
<http://www.usdoj.gov/dea>

**National Clearinghouse for Alcohol
and Drug Information**
P. O. Box 2345
Rockville, MD 20852
(800) 729-6686

National Families in Action
Century Plaza II
2957 Clairmont Road
Suite 150
Atlanta, GA 30329
(404) 248-9676
<http://www.emory.edu/NFIA/>

glossary

acquired immunodeficiency syndrome (AIDS)—A deadly disorder of the immune system. It lowers the body's ability to fight off infectious bacteria and viruses. The cause of AIDS is unknown.

addict—A person who is dependent on a substance.

anabolic steroids—Synthetic steroids that increase muscle size and strength.

black market—An illegal market, or the illegal selling and buying of products or services.

blending—Mixing different drugs.

buffed—Having large muscles.

bulking up—Increasing muscle mass through steroids.

carbohydrates—A class of food that includes sugars and starches. Carbohydrates are the main source of energy for animals.

chemotherapy—A series of drug treatments used to destroy cancer cells.

corticosteroids—Synthetic steroids used to treat some health problems.

cycle—The eight-to-twelve-week period when steroids are used. After that, the user lets his or her body rest for the same period.

doping—A slang term for using steroids to improve athletic performance.

hormones—Naturally produced chemical substances that regulate functions in the body such as growth, sexual development, and reproduction.

human immunodeficiency virus (HIV)—The virus that is believed by many researchers to be the cause of AIDS.

injection—The use of a needle to force a liquid into the body.

juiced—A slang term that describes someone who is taking steroids.

megadosing—Taking large amounts of steroids.

plateau—The point at which a steroid no longer works the way it once did.

prescription—Medication that is bought and sold with a doctor's written instructions.

roid rage—A slang term for uncontrolled anger, frustration, or combativeness that results from using anabolic steroids.

roider—A slang term for a steroid user who takes the drug only for appearance. Other terms for roider are *juicer* and *joy rider*.

shotgunning—A slang term for taking steroids irregularly.

stacking—A slang term for taking several different steroids at the same time.

sterile—Unable to reproduce.

steroids—Chemical substances that regulate functions in the body such as growth. Hormones are one type of steroid.

synthetic—Made from chemicals in a laboratory.

tapering—Slowly decreasing the use of steroids.

tendons—Tissues that attach muscles to bones.

testosterone—A hormone that causes a boy's body to develop.

withdrawal—The process of ridding the body of a drug.

further reading

Lucas, Scott E. *Steroids*. Springfield, N.J.: Enslow Publishers Inc., 1994.

Monroe, Judy. "Steroid Substitutes." *Current Health 2*, April 1996.

Nardo, Don. *Drugs and Sports*. San Diego, Calif.: Lucent Books, 1990.

National Institute on Drug Abuse. *Anabolic Steroids: A Threat to Body and Mind*. Washington, D.C.: U.S. Department of Health and Human Services, 1994.

Peck, Rodney G. *Drugs and Sports*. New York: Rosen Publishing Group, 1992.

Rogak, Lisa Angowski. *Steroids: Dangerous Game*. Minneapolis, Minn.: Lerner Publications, 1992.

Substance Abuse and Mental Health Services Administration. *Tips for Teens: Steroids*. Washington, D.C.: U.S. Department of Health and Human Services.

Talmadge, Katherine S. *Drugs and Sports*. Frederick, Md.: Twenty-First Century Books, 1991.

Internet Addresses

Anabolic Steroids
<http://www.drugfreeamerica.org/steroids.html>

National Institute on Drug Abuse Report—Steroids
<http://www.nida.nih.gov/ResearchReports/Steroids/AnabolicSteroids5.html>

index